NOT GUILTY
AT NUREMBERG

The German Defense Case

Carlos Whitlock Porter

NOT GUILTY AT NUREMBERG
The German Defense Case

By Carlos Whitlock Porter

(c) 2018 by Carlos Whitlock Porter. All rights reserved.
ISBN 978-1-59364-053-8

http://www.cwporter.com

Liberty Bell Publications
P.O. Box 890
York, SC 29745

Contents

INTRODUCTION 5
MARTIN BORMANN 7
CRIMINAL ORGANIZATIONS 8
DOCUMENTS 11
KARL DÖNITZ 15
HANS FRANK 17
WILHELM FRICK 18
HANS FRITZSCHE 20
WALTER FUNK 21
KURT GERSTEIN 23
G.M. GILBERT 24
HERMANN GÖRING 25
RUDOLF HESS 28
RUDOLF HÖSS 30
JAPANESE WAR CRIMES TRIALS 37
ALFRED JODL 40
ERNST KALTENBRUNNER 42
WILHELM KEITEL 45
CONSTANTIN VON NEURATH 47
FRANZ VON PAPEN 49
ERICH RAEDER 51
JOACHIM VON RIBBENTROP 52
ALFRED ROSENBERG AND ERNST SAUCKEL 56
HJALMAR SCHACHT 59
BALDUR VON SCHIRACH 60
ARTHUR SEYSS-INQUART 62
ALBERT SPEER 64
JULIUS STREICHER 65

Prisoner watch, Nuremberg, 1946.

INTRODUCTION

THE RE-WRITING OF HISTORY is as old as history itself.

The Annals of Tacitus, for example, (xv 38), mentions a "rumour" that Nero burned Rome; this "rumour" was repeated by later Roman historians as "fact" (Suetonius, *Nero*, 38; Dio Cassius, *Epistulae*, lxii 16; Pliny, *Naturalis Historia*, xvii 5).

Later writers called this "fact" into question, and demoted the "fact" to mere "rumour".

In 1946, it was a "proven fact" that Nazis made human soap (Judgement, Nuremberg Trial, IMT I 252 [283]; VII 597-600 [656-659]; XIX 506 [566-567]; XXII 496 [564]).

This "fact" has since become, apparently, merely "rumour" (Hilberg, "revised definitive" *Destruction of the European Jews*, Holmes and Meier, NY, page 966: "To this day, the origin of the soap making rumour has not been traced").

The forensically untested "rumour" of Soviet origin (a jar of mysterious stinking material, Exhibit USSR 393) is in the Peace Palace of The Hague. Peace Palace officials show it to eager visitors and tell them it is authentic; but do not, apparently, answer letters from persons asking to have it tested.

In 1943, it was a "rumour" that Nazis were steaming, frying, parboiling, electrocuting, vacuuming and gassing Jews (see, for example, *The Black Book: The Nazi Crime Against the Jewish People*, pp. 270, 274, 280, 313, introduced as "evidence" before the Nuremberg Commission); by 1946, the "gassings" had become "fact", while the steamings, fryings, parboilings, electrocutions and vacuumings remained mere "rumour". (Note: the "steamings" were "proven" in the Pohl Trial, Fourth Nuremberg Trial, NMT IV 1119-1152).

The "evidence" that Nazis "gassed" Jews is qualitatively no better than the "evidence" that they steamed, fried, parboiled, electrocuted, or vacuumed them; it appears legitimate to call this "evidence" into question.

This article contains, not a re-writing of history, but a simple guide to historical material which has been forgotten. The 312,022 notarized defense affidavits presented at the First Nuremberg Trial have been forgotten, while the 8 or 9 prosecution affidavits which "rebutted" them are remembered (XXI 437 [483]).

This article contains a great many references to page numbers. They are not there to confuse, impress, or intimidate the reader, or to prove the truth of the matter stated, but to help interested people find things.

Whether the statements of the defense are more credible than the human soap (Document USSR-197), human hair socks (Document USSR-511), and cannibal hamburgers (Exhibit 1873, Tokyo Trial) of the war crimes prosecutors, is for the reader to decide.

NOTE:

IMT = 1st Nuremberg Trial, in 4 languages.

NMT = 12 later Nuremberg Trials, in English. In the absence of any indication to the contrary, all page numbers refer to the American edition, with the German page numbers in [brackets].

MARTIN BORMANN

Bormann was accused of "persecution of religion" and many other crimes. Bormann's attorney, Dr. Bergold, pointed out that many modern countries (meaning the Soviet Union) are avowedly atheist, and that orders forbidding priests from holding high Party offices (that is, offices in the Nazi Party) could not be called "persecution". In Dr. Bergold's words:

"The party is described as criminal – as a conspiracy. Is it a crime to exclude certain people from membership in a criminal conspiracy? Is that considered a crime?" (V 312 [353]).

Documents were produced in which Bormann prohibited persecution of religion and expressly allowed religion to be taught (XXI 462-465 [512-515]). A condition of this order was that the full Biblical text had to be used; deletions, manipulations or distortions of the text were forbidden. Churches received government subsidies until the end of the war. Due to wartime paper shortages, restrictions were placed upon the printing of all newspapers, not just religious ones (XIX 111-124 [125-139]; XXI 262-263; 346; 534; 539; [292-293; 383; 589; 595]; XXII 40-41 [52-53]).

Bormann's attorney had little difficulty in showing that Bormann could not be convicted of a criminal offense under the laws of any country, since it is clear that stenographers are not criminally responsible for every document they sign. It was not clear to what extent Bormann acted merely as stenographer or secretary. To the prosecution, however, law was irrelevant, and Bormann was sentenced to be hanged. Sentence was to be carried out immediately, ignoring extensive testimony that he had been killed by the explosion of a tank and was unlikely to be in one piece, presenting certain problems of a practical nature (XVII 261-271 [287-297]).

CRIMINAL ORGANIZATIONS

The defense evidence for the "criminal organizations" consists of the testimony of 102 witnesses and 312,022 notarized affidavits (XXII 176 [200]).

The term "criminal" was never defined (XXII 310 [354]; see also XXII 129-135 [148-155]).

Nor was it defined when these organizations became "criminal" (XXII 240 [272-273]).

The Nazi Party itself was criminal dating back to 1920 (XXII 251 [285]) or then again maybe only 1938 (XXII 113 [130]) or maybe even not at all (II 105 [123]).

The 312,022 notarized affidavits were presented to a "commission", and evidence before this "commission" does not appear in the transcript of the Nuremberg Trial. The National Archives in Washington do not possess a copy of the commission transcript, had never heard of it, and do not know what it is.

Of the 312,022 affidavits, only a few dozen were ever translated into English, so the Tribunal could not read them (XXI 287, 397-398 [319, 439]). The President of the Tribunal, Sir Geoffrey Lawrence, understood no German; neither did Robert Jackson.

Due to a last-minute rule change (XXI 437-438, 441, 586-587 [483-485, 488, 645-646]) many more affidavits were rejected on technical grounds (XX 446-448 [487-489]).

The "commission" prepared "summaries" which were presented to the Tribunal (x-thousand affidavits alleging humane treatment of prisoners, etc). These summaries were not considered to be in evidence. The Tribunal promised to read the 312,022 affidavits before arriving at their verdict (XXI 175 [198]); 14 days later it was announced that the 312,022 affidavits were not true (XXII 176-178 [200-203]).

Then a single affidavit from the prosecution (Document D-973) was deemed to have "rebutted" 136,000 affidavits from the defense (XXI 588; 437, 366 [647, 483-484, 404]).

The 102 witnesses were forced to appear and testify before the "commission" before appearing before the Tribunal. Then, 29 of these witnesses (XXI 586 [645]), or 22 of these witnesses (XXII 413 [468]) were allowed to appear before the Tribunal, but their testimony was not permitted to be "cumulative", that is, repetitive of their testimony before the "commission" (XXI 298, 318, 361 [331, 352, 398-399]).

Then, six affidavits from the prosecution were deemed to have "rebutted" the testimony of the 102 witnesses (XXI 153 [175], XXII 221 [251]).

One of these affidavits was in Polish, so the defense could not read it (XX 408 [446]). Another was signed by a Jew named Szloma Gol who claimed to have dug up and cremated 80,000 bodies, including that of his own brother (XXI 157 [179], XXII 220 [250]).

(In the British transcript he has only dug up 67,000 bodies). The prosecution had already rested its case when this occurred (XX 389-393, 464 [426-430, 506]; XXI 586-592 [645-651]). The prosecution then claimed in its final summation that 300,000 affidavits had been presented to the Tribunal and had been considered during the trial, giving the impression that these are prosecution documents (XXII 239 [272]).

In fact, the prosecution got through the entire trial with no more than a few really important affidavits of their own. (See, for example, XXI 437 [483], where eight or nine affidavits were presented for the prosecution against three hundred thousand for the defense; see also XXI 200 [225]; 477-478 [528-529]; 585-586 [643-645]; 615 [686-687]).

In the various concentration camp trials, such as the Trial of Martin Gottfried Weiss, a simpler expedient was agreed upon: mere employment in the camp, even if only for a few weeks, was deemed to constitute "constructive knowledge" of the "Common Plan". "Common Plan", of course, was not defined. It was not necessary to allege specific acts of mistreatment, or to show that anyone had died as a result of mistreatment. (36 of the 40 defendants were sentenced to death.) The term "conspiracy" was usually avoided to simplify the trial procedure.

The transcript of the Nuremberg commission is in The Hague, and fills half of one fire-proof floor-to-ceiling vault. The testimony of each witness was typed with a pagination beginning with page 1, then retyped, with consecutive pagination running to many thousands of pages.

The first drafts and clean copy are in folders, together, stapled, on very brittle paper, with rusty staples. It is absolutely certain that, at least at The Hague, no one has ever read this material.

Summation relating to the testimony of the 102 witnesses appears mostly in fine print in volumes XXI and XXII in the Nuremberg Trial transcript. The fine print means that the passages were deleted from the final defense summation (otherwise the trial would have been much too long). This material runs to several hundred pages. In the transcript published in the United Kingdom, every word of this material is gone. In English, 11 pages in fine print are missing between paragraphs 1 and

2 on page 594 from volume XXI. These appear in the German volumes (XXI 654-664). Most of the rest of it appears to be there.

The material covers, for example:
- Total War XIX 25 [32]
- Reparations XIX 224-232 [249-259]
- German trade unions XXI 462 [512]
- Gestapo and concentration camps XXI 494-530 [546-584]
- Röhm Putsch XXI 576-592 [635-651]
- Crystal Night XXI 590-592 [649-651]
- Resettlement XXI 467-469, 599-603 [517-519, 669-674]
- SD XXII 19-35 [27-47]
- Armaments XXII 62-64 [75-78]

The 312,022 affidavits are probably on deposit with a German archive.

The judgment of the Nuremberg trial is printed twice, in Volumes I and XXII. It is important to obtain the German volumes and read the judgment in volume XXII in German.

Bad German, mistranslations, etc, written by the Americans have been corrected, with footnotes.

Mistakes of this kind in documents may be taken as proof of forgeries.

Generally, the German IMT volumes are preferable to the American ones. Frequent footnotes throughout these volumes alert the reader to mistranslations, missing documents, and falsified copies (for example, XX 205 of the German volumes: "This phrase does not appear in the original document.").

The German volumes are available in paperback from Delphin Verlag, Munich (ISBN 3.7735.2509.5).

(Transcript only; transcript and document volumes in English are available from Oceana Publications, Dobbs Ferry NY, on microfilm).

DOCUMENTS

The standard version of events is that the Allies examined 100,000 documents and chose 1,000 which were introduced into evidence, and that the original documents were then deposited in the Peace Palace at The Hague. This is rather inexact.

The documents used in evidence at Nuremberg consisted largely of "photocopies" of "copies". Many of these original documents were written entirely on plain paper without handwritten markings of any kind, by unknown persons. Occasionally, there is an illegible initial or signature of a more or less unknown person certifying the document as a "true copy".

Sometimes there are German stamps, sometimes not. Many have been "found" by the Russians, or "certified authentic" by Soviet War Crimes Commissions.

Volume XXXIII, a document volume taken at random, contains 20 interrogations or affidavits, 12 photocopies, 5 unsigned copies, 5 original documents with signatures, 4 copies of printed material, 3 mimeographed copies, 3 teletypes, 1 microfilm copy, 1 copy signed by somebody else and 1 unspecified.

The Hague has few, if any, original documents. The Hague has many original post-war "affidavits", or sworn statements, the Tribunal Commission transcripts, and much valuable defense material.

They have the "human soap", which has never been tested, and the "original human soap recipe" (Document USSR-196), which is a forgery; but apparently no original wartime German documents.

The Hague has negative photostats of these documents, on extremely brittle paper which has been stapled. To photocopy the photostats, the staples are removed. When they are re-stapled more holes are made. Most of these documents have not been photocopied very often, and officials at the Hague say it is very unusual for anyone to ask to see them.

The National Archives in Washington (see Telford Taylor's *Use of Captured German and Related Documents*, A National Archive Conference) claim that the original documents are in The Hague. The Hague claims the original documents are in the National Archives.

The Stadtarchiv Nürnberg and the Bundesarchiv Koblenz also have no original documents, and both say the original documents are in Washington.

Since the originals are, in most cases, "copies", there is often no proof that the documents in question ever existed.

Robert Jackson got the trial off to a start by quoting the following forged or otherwise worthless documents: 1947-PS; 1721-PS; 1014-PS; 81-PS; 212-PS; and many others (II 120-142 [141-168]).

1947-PS is a "copy" of a "translation" of a letter from General Fritsch to the Baroness von Schutzbar-Milchling. The Baroness later signed an affidavit stating that she never received the letter in question (XXI 381 [420-421]).

The falsified "letter" from General Fritsch to the Baroness von Schutzbar-Milchling was recognized as such during the trial and is not included in the document volumes, where it should appear at XXVIII 44. Jackson was not, however, admonished by the Tribunal (XXI 380 [420]).

The enthusiastic Americans apparently forged 15 of these "translations", after which the original documents all disappeared (See Taylor, *Captured Documents*).

1721-PS is a forgery in which an SA man writes a report to himself about how he is carrying out an order which is quoted verbatim in the report. Handwritten markings on pages 2 and 3 are obvious imitations of handwritten markings on page 1 (XXI 137-141 [157-161]; 195-198 [219-224]; 425 [470]; XXII 147-150 [169-172]. See also *Testimony Before the Commission*, Fust, 25 April, and Lutze, 7 May 1946). The National Archives have a positive photostat of 1721-PS, and The Hague has a negative photostat. The "original" is a photocopy (XXVII 485).

1014-PS is a falsified "Hitler Speech" written on plain paper by an unknown person. The document bears the heading "Second Speech" although it is known that Hitler gave only one speech on that date. There are four versions of this speech, 3 of them forgeries: 1014-PS, 798-PS, L-3, and an authentic version, Ra-27 (XVII 406-408 [445-447]; XVIII 390-402 [426-439]).

The third forgery, Document L-3, bears an FBI laboratory stamp and was never even accepted into evidence (II 286 [320-321]), but 250 copies of it were given to the press as authentic (II 286-293 [320-328]).

This document is quoted by A.J.P. Taylor on page 254 of *The Origins of the Second World War* (Fawcett Paperbacks, 2nd Edition, with Answer to his Critics) giving his source as *German Foreign Policy*, Series D vii, No 192 and 193.

L-3 is the source of many statements attributed to Hitler, particularly "who today remembers the fate of the Armenians?" and "our enemies are little worms, I saw them at Munich". "Hitler" also compares himself to Genghis Khan and says he will exterminate the Poles, and kick Chamberlain in the groin in front of the photographers. The document appears to have been prepared on the same typewriter as many other Nuremberg documents, including the two other versions of the same speech. This typewriter was probably a Martin from the Triumph-Adler-Werke, Nuremberg.

81-PS is a "certified true copy" of an unsigned letter on plain paper prepared by an unknown person. If authentic, it is the first draft of a letter never sent. This is invariably spoken of as a letter written by Rosenberg, which Rosenberg denied (XI 510-511 [560-561]). The document lacks signature, initial, blank journal number (a bureaucratic marking) and was not found among the papers of the person to whom it was addressed (XVII 612 [664]). 81-PS is a "photocopy" with a Soviet exhibit number (USSR-353, XXV 156-161).

212-PS was also prepared by an unknown person, entirely on plain paper, without any handwritten markings, date, address, or stamp (III 540 [602], XXV 302-306; see also photocopies of negative photostats from The Hague).

This is, unfortunately, only typical. Document 386-PS, the "Hossbach Protokoll", Hitler's supposed speech of 5 November 1938, is a certified photocopy of a microfilm copy of a re-typed "certified true copy" prepared by an American, of a re-typed "certified true copy" prepared by a German, of unauthenticated handwritten notes by Hossbach, of a speech by Hitler, written from memory 5 days later. This is not the worst document, but one of the best, because we know who made one of the copies. The text of 386-PS has been "edited" (XLII 228-230).

Thus "trial by document" works as follows: A, an unknown person, listens to alleged "oral statements" made by B, and takes notes or prepares a document on the basis of those alleged oral statements. The document is then introduced into evidence, not against A, who made the copy, but against B, C, D, E and a host of other people, although there is nothing to connect them with the document or the alleged statements. It is casually stated as fact that "B said", or that "C did", or that "D and E knew". This is contrary to the rules of evidence of all civilised countries. Nor are the documents identified by witnesses.

The forgery of original documents was rarely resorted to at Nuremberg, because the documents were not brought to court. The "original document" – that is, the original unsigned "copy" – was kept in a safe in the Document Centre (II 195 [224], 256-258 [289-292]).

Then, 2 "photocopies" of the "copy" (V 21 [29]) or 6 photocopies (II 251-253 [284-286]) were prepared and brought to court. All other copies were re-typed on a mimeograph using a stencil (IX 504 [558-559]).

In the transcript, the word "original" is used to mean "photocopy" (II 249-250 [283-284]; XIII 200 [223], 508 [560], 519 [573], XV 43 [53], 169 [189] 171 [191] 327 [359]), to distinguish the photocopies from the mimeograph copies (IV 245-246 [273-274]).

"Translations" of all documents were available from the beginning of the trial (II 159-160 [187-189], 191 [219-220], 195 [224], 215 [245], 249-250 [282-283], 277 [312], 415 [458], 437 [482-483]), but the "original" German texts were not available until at least two months later. This applies not just to the trial briefs and indictment, etc. but to ALL DOCUMENTS.

The defense received no documents in German until after January 9, 1946 (V 22-26 [31-35]).

Documents which appear to have been prepared on the same typewriter include Document 3803-PS, a letter from Kaltenbrunner to the Mayor of Vienna, and the cover letter from this same Mayor sending Kaltenbrunner's letter to the Tribunal (XI 345-348 [381-385]). This letter from Kaltenbrunner contains a false geographical term (XIV 416 [458]).

KARL DÖNITZ

Dönitz was imprisoned for waging "illegal submarine warfare" against the British. In international law, everything is a matter of reciprocity and international agreements, which can only be enforced through reciprocity. In warfare, the best defense against a weapon is a vigorous counterattack with the same weapon. The British, due to their mastery of the seas, fought both world wars through blockade, and the so-called Navicert system. Neutral ships were stopped at sea, and forced to pull into British ports where they were searched according to complicated formulae: if a neutral country imported more food, fertilizer, wool, leather, rubber, cotton, etc. than the quantities believed necessary for its own consumption (in the opinion of the British), the difference was assumed to be intended for reshipment to the Germans.

Result: the ship (and entire cargo) was confiscated and sold at auction, which also violated the clauses of all British marine insurance contracts.

In 1918-19, the blockade was maintained for 8 months after the Armistice to force the Germans to ratify the Versailles Treaty. Hundreds of thousands of Germans died of starvation after the war while the diplomats delayed, an obvious violation of the conditions of the Armistice and all international law. This is what Hitler correctly termed "the greatest breach of faith of all time". The British point of view appears to be that the blockade was legal but was carried out in a totally illegal manner (see *1911 Encyclopaedia Britannica*, "Neutrality", *1922 Encyclopaedia Britannica*, "Blockade", "Peace Conference"). In the war against Japan, the Americans "sank everything that moved since the first day of the war".

Neutrals, including the United States, complained that this violated their neutrality, but complied, again, in violation of their own neutrality. A nation which allows its neutrality to be violated may be treated as a belligerent.

The British never ratified the Fifth Hague Convention of 18 October 1907 on the Rights of Neutrals, but considered its terms binding on the Germans and Japanese, despite an all-participation clause (i.e., the convention ceases to apply if a non-signatory participates in the conflict).

In 1939, the Germans possessed only 26 Atlantic-going submarines, one fifth of the French total alone. Moreover, German submarines were much smaller than those of other nations. A counter-blockade against the British could only be enforced by warning neutrals not to sail in waters surrounding the British Isles. To the British, this was a "crime".

Of these 26 submarines, many were, at any one time, under repair; so that during some months only 2 or 3 were seaworthy. It is obvious that submarines cannot carry out search and seizure in the same manner as a surface navy; a submarine, once it has surfaced, is almost defenseless against the smallest gun mounted on a merchant vessel, not to mention radio, radar, and aircraft.

It was demanded by the British at Nuremberg that German submarines should have surfaced, notified the surface vessel of their intention to search; waited for the surface vessel to commence hostilities; then sink the vessel, presumably with the submarine's deck guns; then take the dozens of hundreds of survivors on board the submarine (where they would be in far greater danger than in any lifeboat), and take them to the nearest land.

When British aircraft appeared and sank the submarine, killing the survivors, they had, of course, been "murdered" by the Germans. No international convention requires this, and no nation fought in this manner. Since rescuing survivors rendered the submarine unfit for duty and frequently resulted in the loss of submarine and crew, Doenitz prohibited any act of rescue. This was called an order to "exterminate survivors". This was not upheld in the judgment, however.

Doenitz was also accused of encouraging the German people to hopeless resistance, a crime also committed by Winston Churchill, Doenitz replied.

"It was very painful that our cities were still being bombed to pieces and that through these bombing attacks and the continued fight more lives were lost. The number of these people is about 300,000 to 400,000, the largest number of whom perished in the bombing of Dresden, which cannot be justified from a military point of view, and which could not have been predicted.

"Nevertheless, this figure is relatively small compared with the millions of German people we would have lost in the East, soldiers and civilians, if we had capitulated in the winter." (XIII 247-406 [276-449]; XVIII 312-372 [342-406])

HANS FRANK

Frank was accused of making hundreds of anti-Semitic statements in a 12,000 page document called his "diary". The "diary" contains only one page signed by Frank, and hundreds of humane statements, which were ignored (XII 115-156 [129-173]). The anti-Semitic statements were selected by the Russians and typeset in a short document which was introduced into evidence as Document 2233-PS, invariably called "Frank's Diary".

The actual "diary" of 12,000 pages consists of summaries (not verbatim transcripts or stenographic notes) of conferences in which 5 or 6 people often spoke at once in circumstances of great confusion; it was not clear to whom which statements should be attributed (XII 86 [97-98]).

Frank gave his "diary" to the Americans in the belief that it would exonerate him; he had protested Hitler's illegality in public speeches at great personal risk, and tried to resign 14 times (XII 2-114 [8-128]; XVIII 129-163 [144-181]).

Frank became convinced that atrocities had occurred after reading about the Soviet Majdanek Trial in the foreign press (XII 35 [43]). Auschwitz was not in territory controlled by Frank.

Frank saw his task as the creation of an independent judiciary in a National Socialist State, a task which he found impossible. In a speech on November 19, 1941, Frank said,

"Law cannot be degraded to a position where it becomes an object of bargaining. Law cannot be sold. It is either there, or it is not there. Law cannot be marketed on the stock exchange. If the law finds no support, then the State too loses its moral stay and sinks into the depths of night and horror."

Hitler's illegalities never included the passing of an ex post facto law; in 3 cases, punishment was increased retroactively (XVII 504 [547]).

Frank's alleged looting of art treasures will be discussed together with that of Rosenberg.

WILHELM FRICK

Frick was hanged for "Germanizing" the inhabitants of Posen, Danzig, West Prussia, Eupen, Malmedy, the Sudetenland, the Memelland, and Austria. With the exception of Austria, these were former parts of the Prussian Reich, separated from Germany by the Versailles Treaty. Malmedy is French-speaking – the other areas are all German speaking. Austria was unable to subsist as an economic unit after 1919, and had demanded to be united with Germany by vote. The Allied victors responded by threatening to cut off all food supplies (XVIII 55 [66], XIX 360 [397]).

Another crime committed by Frick was killing 275,000 feebleminded persons, according to the "report" of a Czech "War Crimes Commission".

Frick, like Göring, was accused of responsibility for the existence of the concentration camps. In Frick's defense it was pointed out that "protective custody" pre-dated the National Socialist accession to power in both Germany and Austria. In Austria, it was called Anhaltehaft, and was used to imprison thousands of National Socialists (XXI 518-521 [572-576]). "Protective custody" exists in West Germany today and is called U-haft.

In the final judgment of one of the most important Dachau Trials (*Trial of Martin Gottfried Weiss and Thirty-Nine Others, Law Reports of Trials of War Criminals*, volume XI, p.15, published by the United Nations), the following sentence appears: "In the Mauthausen Concentration Camp case the facts were basically the same – though the casualty figures were much higher as mass extermination by means of a gas chamber was practised..."

Is this an admission that no gas chamber existed at Dachau? According to *Law Reports of Trials of War Criminals*, no Dachau trial ever "proved" the existence of a gas chamber at Dachau.

At Nuremberg, a "certified true copy" of the judgment of the Trial of Martin Gottfried Weiss and Thirty Nine Others was introduced into evidence with that sentence deleted as Document 3590-PS (V 199 [228]) along with 3 other documents alleging mass extermination by gassing at Dachau (Document 3249-PS, V 172-173 [198], XXXII 60; Document 2430-PS, XXX 470; and 159-L, XXXVII 621).

Frick was accused by the deponent of the "mass gassings at Dachau" affidavit, Document 3249-PS, (written by Lt. Daniel L. Margolies, also involved in the forgery of 3 Hitler speeches, XIV 65 [77], and signed by Dr. Franz Blaha) of having visited Dachau. Frick denied this, and demanded to take the stand to be confronted with Blaha and to testify in his own defense.

This request was denied, and Frick apparently gave up. He never testified. His defense summation appears at XVIII 164-189 [182-211].

The deponent, Dr. Franz Blaha, a Communist, was President of the International Dachau Association in 1961, still claiming to have witnessed mass gassings and to have made trousers and other leather goods out of human skin.

The trial of Martin Gottfried Weiss is available on 6 reels of microfilm (MII 74, National Archives). The pre-trial gas chamber exhibits (report, diagrams, shower nozzle, reel 1) were never introduced into evidence and are missing from the trial exhibits (reel 4). The transcripts (reels 2 & 3) contain no mention of any gas chamber at Dachau except for a few sentences in the testimony of Dr Blaha (Volume 1 pp. 166-169). The human skin came from moles (Volume 4, pp. 450, 462, 464).

HANS FRITZSCHE

Fritzsche became convinced from a letter that mass killings were being carried out in Russia and attempted to verify this. He was, however, unable to find any evidence of it (XVII 172-175 [191-195]). Fritzsche is an important defendant because it was admitted in his case that foreign newspapers printed much false news about Germany (XVII 175-176 [194-196]; see also XVII 22-24 [30-33]). Yet, these same newspaper stories and radio reports constituted the "facts of common knowledge" which the Tribunal alleged needed no proof (Article 21 of rules of evidence, I 15 [16], II 246 [279]).

It was pointed out in Fritzsche's defense that no international convention exists regulating propaganda or atrocity stories, true or false, and that only one national law of one state (Switzerland) made it unlawful to insult foreign Heads of State. That Fritzsche could be guilty of no crime, was, at Nuremberg, simply irrelevant. It was deemed undesirable to have a "trial" in which all defendants were convicted. In the horse-trading which preceded the final verdict, it was agreed that Fritzsche should be released (XVII 135-261 [152-286]; XIX 312-352 [345-388]).

WALTER FUNK

Funk was a classical pianist from a highly respected artistic family, married for 25 years at the time of the trial, and former financial editor. Like most of the defendants, Funk was accused of performing "immoral acts" such as accepting birthday gifts from Hitler, proving "willing participation in the Common Plan". (Obviously, such acts are not illegal.)

Funk claimed that the British and the Poles had conspired to provoke Germany into war in the belief that the generals would overthrow Hitler (XIII 111-112 [125-126]).

Funk was accused of conspiring with the SS to murder concentration camp inmates in order to finance the war effort by pulling their teeth out. The gold teeth were stored in a vault at the Reichsbank, along with shaving kits, fountain pens, large alarm clocks, and other more or less useless junk. Forgotten was Rudolf Höss's testimony that the teeth were melted at Auschwitz (XI 417 [460]).

Funk testified that the amounts and kinds of loot were "absurd" and pointed out that the SS acted as customs police and enforced exchange control regulations, including a prohibition against the ownership of gold, silver, and foreign coins or currency. It was quite natural that the SS should confiscate large amounts of valuables, and that the SS, as a government agency, should have financial accounts, and that these accounts would contain valuables. Germans kept valuables in the same vaults as well, to which the Reichsbank had no access, since they were private safety deposit accounts.

With the increased bombing raids, more and more valuables were deposited in the vaults by ordinary German citizens. Finally, after a particularly damaging raid on the bank, the valuables were removed to a potassium mine in Thuringen. The Americans found the valuables there, and falsified a film of it. Funk and his attorney showed the falsity of the film using an opposing witness, in some of the shrewdest testimony and cross examination in the entire trial (XIII 169 [189-190], 203-204 [227-228], 562-576 [619-636]; XXI 233-245 [262-275]).

Also given short shrift was the ridiculous Oswald Pohl affidavit, Document 4045-PS, in which Funk was accused of discussing the use of gold teeth from dead Jews to finance the war at a dinner party attended by dozens of people, including waiters (XVIII 220-263 [245-291]). This affidavit is in German and is witnessed by Robert Kempner. Pohl was later convicted of "steaming" people to death in 10 "steam chambers" at Treblinka, and making doormats out of their hair (NMT IV 1119-1152) (Fourth National Military Tribunal, Nuremberg).

Funk believed, like other defendants, that crimes had occurred, but maintained that he knew nothing about it. His belief that crimes had occurred does not, in itself, prove that that belief was true.

KURT GERSTEIN

Kurt Gerstein is often referred to as a Holocaust "witness"; however, this is not correct. By "witness", one normally understands a person who has seen something and who appears to testify as to his personal knowledge; Gerstein did not do that. Gerstein was an unworn affiant or deponent, which means that he is simply a name appearing at the end of a "statement", typewritten in French, which he may or may not have written. (Document 1553-PS rejected at Nuremberg) (VI 333-334 [371-372], 362-363 [398-399]).

One of the stories current about Gerstein is that he wrote the statement in Cherche-Midi prison, in France, and committed suicide, after which his body disappeared.

It is far more probable that the statement was written in French by a German Jewish interrogator-"interpreter", and that some of the inconsistencies (such as winter occurring in August, or being in a car in one sentence, and a train in the next) resulted from imperfect transcription of the notes of interrogation into affidavit form. In minor war crimes trials and Japanese war crimes trials, unsworn "statements" of this kind are fairly common, on the theory that they possess "probative value" but less "weight" than sworn statements. It is also possible that Gerstein died of injuries sustained during "interrogation"; or perhaps he hanged himself with the typewriter ribbon.

This document was later extensively quoted in the Pohl Trial, where it was "proven" that Treblinka had 10 "gas chambers" (1553-PS) and 10 "steam chambers" (3311-PS) in the same camp at the same time.

G.M. GILBERT

One of the most famous accounts of the behavior and psychology of the Nuremberg Trial defendants is that of the German-born psychologist, G.M. Gilbert, in his book *Nuremberg Diary*. Much of the material consists of conversations which the defendants and other persons, such as Rudolf Höss, allegedly had with Gilbert or each other (!) and which Gilbert allegedly wrote down from memory afterwards.

A comparison of texts with the Nuremberg trial transcript will show that the defendants did not speak in the style attributed to them by Gilbert. Gilbert took no notes. No witnesses were present.

Persons who believe that Documents 1014-PS, 798-PS, and L-3 are "Hitler speeches", at least in comparison with Document Ra-27, may continue believing that Gilbert's book contains "statements of the Nuremberg Trial defendants". This does not rule out, of course, that they may have made statements similar to those allegedly "remembered" by Gilbert.

Gilbert believed that the defendants gassed millions of Jews. If they felt no guilt for their actions, this proved that they were "schizoid".

It is obvious that such a belief on Gilbert's part would influence his perception and memory to some extent, even if he is telling the truth as he remembers it. If he lied, he was not the only "American" at Nuremberg who did so. Telford Taylor, for example, was incapable of repeating the simplest statement truthfully. (See XX 626 [681-682], the statements of General Manstein, compared with Taylor's "quotation" from Manstein, XXII 276 [315]).

Gilbert's dishonesty is best proven by the entry for December 14, 1945:

"Major Walsh continued reading documentary evidence of the extermination of the Jews at Treblinka and Auschwitz. A Polish document stated: 'All victims had to strip off their clothes and shoes, which were collected afterwards, whereupon all victims, women and children first, were driven into the death chambers... small children were simply thrown inside' " (p.69, 1st edition).

The "documentary evidence" is, of course, a Communist "War Crimes Report" and the "death chambers", of course, are "steam chambers" (III 567-568 [632-633]).

HERMANN GÖRING

Göring was accused of creating the concentration camp system and plotting "aggressive war" against Poland. Göring's defense was that Germany was a sovereign state, recognized by every government in the world (XXI 580-581 [638-639]); that Hitler was legally elected; that every nation has the right to legislate and to organize its affairs as it sees fit; that General von Schleicher had attempted to rule illegally and unconstitutionally without the support of the National Socialists; that Germany was on the verge of civil war in 1933; that concentration camps were invented by the British during the Boer War, and that internment of aliens and political opponents was practiced by both Britain and the United States during WWII.

The order to create the camps was unquestionably legal under an emergency clause in the Weimar Constitution, and was signed by Hindenburg (Reich President's Decree of 28 February 1933), under the authority of Article 48, paragraph 2, of the Weimar Constitution (XVII 535 [581], XIX 357 [394]).

According to a prosecution document, Document R-129 (III 506 [565-566])) there were 21,400 inmates in all German concentration camps put together in 1939. 300,000 persons were confined in ordinary prisons (XVII 535-536 [581-582], XX 159 [178]).

One year after the war, 300,000 Germans were held in Allied prison camps under "automatic arrest" clauses in Allied agreements (such as Point B-5 of the Joint Declaration of Potsdam)(XVIII 52 [62]).

The majority of prisoners in German concentration camps were Communists and common criminals (XVII 535-536 [581-582], XXI 516-521 [570-576], 607-614 [677-685]).

During the war, due to the Allied blockade, the camp system was expanded to utilize the labour of enemy aliens, criminals, Jehovah's Witnesses and Communists. It was pointed out that America imprisoned 11,000 Jehovah's Witnesses (XI 513 [563]).

Britain fought both world wars in defiance of international law by reducing Germany and any occupied territories to literal starvation through blockade (XIII 445-450 [492-497]; XVIII 334-335 [365-367]). It was this which necessitated requisitions and labour conscription in occupied territories, legal under Article 52 of The Fourth Hague Convention on Land Warfare 18 October 1907. It was this which made people happy to work in Germany and remit wages to their families (between two and three billion Reichsmarks during the war).

The "slaves" paid German taxes on their wages, and were disciplined through fines, which could not exceed a week's wages (V 509 [571]). For gross indiscipline, they could be sent to a work camp (not a concentration camp) for a period not exceeding 56 days (XXI 521 [575-576]). It was strictly forbidden to beat or mistreat them.

Prisoners of war could volunteer to be released from prisoner of war camps and work in industry, in which case they were treated like any other industrial workers (XVIII 496-498 [542-544]), but lost protection under the Geneva Prisoner of War Convention. They could not be forced to do so.

The Vichy Regime in France obtained the release and immediate return home of 1 prisoner of war for every 3 workers sent to Germany under contract for a period of 6 months (XVIII 497 [543]). It was not possible to violate the Geneva Prisoner of War Convention by forcing French, Belgian or Dutch prisoners to participate in hostilities against their own countries, because their own countries were no longer fighting (XVIII 472-473 [516]).

As for the attack on Poland, the Polish crisis existed for over a year prior to the Molotov-Ribbentrop Pact and the German and Soviet attack. During this entire time, the Poles never called for an impartial international Court of Arbitration; never called on the League of Nations; because they did not wish an equitable solution. They were content to continue to violate their international agreements by expelling Polish citizens of German descent, as well as many hundreds of thousands of Jews (XVI 275 [304]).

The influx of Polish Jews into Germany was the principal immediate cause of German anti-Semitism, according to many defendants and defense witnesses (XXI 134-135 [155]; XXII 148 [169]). Polish Jews were involved in many financial scandals and swindling schemes, such as the Barnat-Kutitsky affair (XXI 569 [627]).

As for "conspiracy to wage war in defiance of the laws of war", of course it was the British who did that, with mass aerial bombings. German soldiers went into battle with detailed written instructions that property was to be respected; prisoners must be humanely treated; women must be respected; and so on (IX 57-58 [68-69], 86 [100-101], XVII 516 [560]).

Frequent trials resulting in many death penalties against Germans were carried out by the German armed forces against members of their own armed forces for rape or looting, even if the value of the property involved was slight (XVIII 368 [401-402], XXI 390 [431], XXII 78 [92]). Requisition of government property was legal under the Hague Convention. The Soviet Union was not a signatory to this convention. In any case, in Communist countries there was no private property. Göring said he had been to Russia, and the people there had nothing to steal (IX 349-351 [390-393]). Furthermore, the Allies were presently engaged in everything they accused the Germans of doing (XXI 526 [581]; XXII 366-367 [418-420]).

Göring demolished the "pressure chamber medical experiment" accusation by saying that every airman had to test his physical reactions to high altitude; there was nothing sinister about a so-called "pressure chamber" (XXI 304-310 [337-344]). Americans carried out medical experiments resulting in death while the Nuremberg trial was still going on (XIX 90-92 [102-104]; see also XXI 356, 370 [393, 409]). Ironically, it was alleged that "defensive war" included preventive attack (XXII 448 [508]) or to protect citizens of a foreign country from their own government (XIX 472 [527]; XXII 37 [49]), except when Germans did it (X 456 [513]). Protests that Germans did just that were ignored. The Soviets had 10,000 tanks and 150 divisions massed along the border of eastern Poland, and had increased the number of airports in their section of the country from 20 to 100. Detailed maps were later found which would not have been necessary for defensive purposes. It was believed that to await an attack upon the oil fields of Romania or the coal fields of Silesia would be suicidal (XIX 13-16 [20-23], XX 578 [630-631]; XXII 71 [85]). It seems unlikely that nations with vast colonial empires (Britain, France) or claims upon entire hemispheres (the United States) could agree upon a workable definition of "aggressive war". Indeed it was admitted in the judgment of Nuremberg that "defense", "aggression", and "conspiracy" were never defined (XXII 464, 467 [527, 531]). No doubt "defensive war" is the medieval "bellum justum" dressed up in liberal jargon (IX 236-691 [268-782]; XVII 516-550 [560-597]; XXI 302-317 [335-351]).

RUDOLF HESS

According to the report of Robert H. Jackson, (quoted by Judge Bert A. Röling of the Tokyo Tribunal, writing in *A Treatise on International Criminal Law*, vol. 1., pp. 590-608, edited by M. Cherif Bassiouni and Ved. F. Nanda, Chas Thomas Publisher), the British, French, and Soviets at Nuremberg did not wish to charge the Germans with "aggressive war" at all, for obvious reasons. This accusation was invented by the Americans for the sole, express, and admitted purpose of justifying American violations of international law. These violations of international law would include the Lend  Lease Program; convoying and repairing British wartime ships for two years prior to Pearl Harbor; allowing British ships to disguise themselves as American while the U.S. was officially neutral; the illegal declaration of a 300 mile limit; the occupation of Iceland; reporting the movements of German and Italian submarines; bombing and ramming attacks against German and Italian submarines beginning as early as July of 1941, and other actions obviously indicative of "aggressive war".

Thus Hess was imprisoned for 47 years not only for actions which were not illegal (attempting to stop the war, save millions of lives and prevent the destruction of Europe and the British Empire), but for "crimes" which were invented to cover the crimes of his accusers.

It was not alleged at Nuremberg that Germany had committed "aggression" against Britain or France; the question of whether Britain and France had, therefore, committed "aggression" against Germany was left unanswered (IX 473 [525]; XVII 580 [629]). Hess was accused of plotting with Hitler to take Britain out of the war so that Hitler could attack Russia. His defense was that his action was dictated by sincerity; that he knew nothing of any attack on Russia.

Hess's defense summation appears at XIX 353-396 [390-437]. From his final (and only) statement (XXII 368-373 [420-425]) Hess appears to have been a man who could be totally insane one moment, and brilliantly lucid, sane and logical a moment later. It is possible that this condition was acquired in Britain.

RUDOLF HÖSS

Rudolf Höss was the Auschwitz commandant whose "confessions" have "proven" that Hitler gassed six million Jews (or five million, the figure usually used at Nuremberg). His best-known "confession" is the one quoted by William L. Shirer on pages 968-969 of *The Rise and Fall of the Third Reich*.

This document, Document 3868-PS, should be seen in its context. The ex parte written "statement" or affidavit (i.e., prepared in the presence of only one of the parties) was a principal prosecutor's tool in the witchcraft trials of the Middle Ages, only to disappear for several centuries, then reappear in Communist show trials and war crimes trials.

These documents violate many standard rules of legal procedure, such as the rule against asking leading questions, the rule against prior consistent statements (i.e., the multiplication of evidence by repetition; normally, such statements are only admissible when they contradict other statements made later), the right to confront and cross-examine one's accuser, and the privilege against self-incrimination.

Nor would the "evidence" in war crime trials be admissible in a court martial. Even in 1946, the introduction of depositions by the prosecution in capital cases before a court martial was forbidden by Article 25 of the US Articles of War. Article 38 required the use of standard Federal rules of evidence. At Nuremberg, there was never the slightest pretense that Höss wrote this document. If that had been the case, it would not state, "I understand English as it is written above", but rather, "I have written this statement myself".

In the minor trials (Hadamar, Natzweiler, etc.) it is common to find confessions written entirely in the handwriting of the interrogator, in English, with a final statement in the prisoners handwriting, in German, stating that these are his statements and that he is satisfied with the translation into English! Another formula occurs on page 57 of the

Hadamar volume of Sir David Maxwell-Fyfe's book, *War Crimes Trials*, "I certify that the above has been read to me in German, my native tongue" (in English).

The pretense was that the prisoner was interrogated through an interpreter in question and answer form, after which the questions were deleted, and the answers were run together in the form of an affidavit, usually written by a different person from the interrogator who conducted the questioning. At Belsen, for example, every affidavit was written by one officer, Major Smallwood. In this trial, a combination Auschwitz-Belsen trial, the court-appointed British and free Polish defense team demolished the prosecution case – including the "selections for mass gassings" – but were overruled on the grounds that involuntary statements and oral and written hearsay were admissible, "not to convict the innocent, but to convict the guilty" (*Law Reports of Trials of War Criminals*, Vol. II. (This thin volume must be read in its entirety.)) After the affidavit was prepared by the officer who did nothing but write affidavits, it was presented in its finished form to the prisoner for signature. If it was not signed, it was introduced into evidence anyway.

Objections went to "weight", in the jargon of war crimes proceedings, rather than to "admissibility". An example of an unsigned affidavit by Rudolf Höss is Document NO-4498-B. The B means that this document is a "translation" with typewritten signature of an "original" document, Document NO-4498-A, written in Polish, and allegedly signed by Höss.

There is also a Document NO-4498-C, in English. Affidavits A and C are not attached to Affidavit B, the "true copy". Document 3868-PS, quoted by Shirer, was signed in English, 3 times, but not in the "translation" into German. The document contains a minor change initialled by Höss, with a small "h", and an entire sentence written entirely in the interrogator's handwriting (compare capital "W"s) not initialled by Höss. The initial, of course, is there to "prove" that he has "read and corrected" the document. The content of this handwritten sentence is refuted elsewhere (XXI 529 [584]).

When the affidavit was presented to the prisoner, it was sometimes corrected extensively, leading to two or more versions of the same document. In these cases, the longer ones are "quoted", and the shorter ones are "lost". An example of this practice is Document D-288, the affidavit of Dr. Wilhelm Jäger, cited pp. 948-949 of Shirer's *Rise and Fall of the Third Reich* (see Albert Speer.) Jäger testified that he signed 3 or 4 copies of the same document, a much shorter one. The shorter one was originally presented against the elder Krupp, before charges against him were dropped. In this document, the longer one, the translation into English is dated prior to the signature date on the "original". Jäger's court appearance was an unmitigated disaster, but that is forgotten (XV 264-283 [291-312]).If the affiant appeared to testify, he invariably contradicted the affidavit, but contradictions are ignored.

Other affidavit signers whose court appearances were catastrophic include General Westhoff, who contradicted his unsworn "statement" 27 times (XI 155-189 [176-212]); and a "germ warfare witness", Schreiber (XXI 547-562 [603-620]); Paul Schmidt's affidavit (Schmidt was Hitler's interpreter), Document 3308-PS – presented to him for signature when he was too sick to read it carefully – was partially repudiated by him (X 222 [252]), but used in evidence against Von Neurath, despite Schmidt's repudiation (XVI 381 [420-421] XVII 40-41 [49-50]). Ernst Sauckel signed an affidavit written prior to his arrival at Nuremberg (XV 64-68 [76-80]) and signed under duress (his wife and 10 children were to be handed over to the Poles or Russians).

Since the affiants almost never (if ever) wrote their own "statements", it is common to find identical or nearly identical phrases or even entire paragraphs occurring in different documents, even when they have been prepared on different days by supposedly different people; for example, affidavits 3 and 5 of Blaskovitz and Halder (Exhibits 536-US and 537-US); Documents USSR-471 and USSR-472 and 473; and Documents USSR-264 and 272 (human soap affidavits).

Other affidavits signed by Höss include Document NO-1210, in which the English was written first, with extensive interpolations, additions and corrections, including 2 different first drafts of page 4, and 2 different first drafts of page 5, then translated into German and signed by Höss. That is, the "translation" is the "original", and the "original" is the "translation".

Document 749(b)D was "translated orally" into German from English for Höss prior to signature. The signature is faint to the point of illegibility, indicating possible ill health, fatigue or torture. The torture has been described by Rupert Butler in *Legions of Death* (Hamlyn Paperbacks) The "confession" quoted by Sir David Maxwell-Fyfe on April Fool's Day, April 1, 1946, in which Höss "confessed" to killing 4 million Jews (X 389 [439-440]), instead of the usual 2.5 million of April 5, 1946, has either never existed or has gotten "lost".

It is not true that Höss' court appearance at Nuremberg consisted chiefly of assenting to his affidavit; this is true only of his cross-examination by Col. John Amen of the U.S. Army. Instead, Höss appeared to testify, and, as usual, contradicted his affidavit and himself as much as possible (XI 396-422 [438-466]). For example, where the affidavit states (XI 416 [460]) "we knew when the people were dead because their screaming stopped", (a crudely obvious toxicological impossibility), his oral testimony claims (XI 401 [443]), in response to grossly improper leading questions posed by Kaltenbrunner's "defense attorney"), that the people became unconscious; leaving unsolved the problem of just how he knew when they were, in fact, dead. He forgot to mention that killing insects with Zyklon-B took two days, a fact he mentioned elsewhere (Document NI-036, p. 3, German text, answer to Question 25, and *Kommandant in Auschwitz*, p. 155). With such a slow-acting poison, the people would suffocate first.

Höss claimed that the order to kill the Jews of Europe was given orally (XI 398 [440]), but that orders to keep the killings secret were given in writing (XI 400 [442]. He claimed that persons were cremated in pits at Auschwitz, a notorious swamp (XI 420 [464]), and that gold teeth were melted down on the spot (XI 417 [460]), but an evacuation of the concentration camps to avoid capture would have led to unnecessary deaths (XI 407 [449-450]), and, almost, that there was no killing program at all! This is worth quoting:

"Until the outbreak of war in 1939, the situation in the camps regarding feeding, accommodation, and treatment of detainees, was the same as in any other prison or penitentiary in the Reich. The detainees were treated strictly, yes, but methodical beatings or ill-treatment were out of the question. The Reichsführer gave frequent warnings that every SS man who laid violent hands on a detainee would be punished; and quite often SS men who did ill-treat detainees were punished. Feeding and accommodation at that time were in every respect put on the same basis as that of other prisoners under legal administration. The accommodation in the camps during those years was still normal because the mass influxes at the outbreak of and during the war had as yet not taken place. When the war started and when mass deliveries of political detainees arrived, and, later on, when detainees, who were members of resistance movements, arrived from the occupied territories, the construction of buildings and the extensions of the camps could no longer keep up with the number of detainees who arrived.

"During the first years of the war this problem could still be overcome by improvising measures; but, later, due to the exigencies of the war, this was no longer possible, since there were practically no building materials any longer at our disposal [Note: the bodies are supposed to have been burnt using wood for fuel.]...

"This led to a situation where detainees in the camps no longer had sufficient powers of resistance against the ensuing plagues and epidemics... the aim wasn't to have as many dead as possible or to destroy as many detainees as possible. The Reichsführer was constantly concerned with the problems of engaging all forces possible in the armament industry...

"These so-called ill-treatments and torturing in concentration camps, stories of which were spread everywhere amongst the people, and particularly by detainees who were liberated by the occupying armies, were not, as assumed, inflicted methodically, but by individual leaders, sub-leaders, and men who laid violent hands on them...

"If in any way such a matter was brought to my notice, the perpetrator was, of course, immediately relieved of his post or transferred somewhere else. So that, even if he wasn't punished because there wasn't evidence to prove his guilt, he was taken away and given another position...

"The catastrophic situation at the end of the war was due to the fact that as a result of the destruction of railways and of the continuous bombings of the industrial works, it was no longer possible to properly care for these masses, for example, at Auschwitz, with its 140,000 detainees. Improvised measures, truck columns, and everything else tried by the commandants to improve the situation, were of little or no avail. The number of sick became immense. There were next to no medical supplies; plagues raged everywhere.

"Detainees who were capable of work were used continuously by order of the Reichsführer, even half-sick people had to be used wherever possible in industry. As a result, every bit of space in the concentration camps which could possibly be used for lodging was filled with sick and dying detainees.

"At the end of the war, there were still thirteen concentration camps. All the other points which are marked here on the map means so-called labour camps attached to the armament factories situated there...

"If any ill-treatment of detainees by guards occurred – I myself have never observed any – then this was possible only to a very small degree, since all officers in charge of the camps took care that as few SS men as possible had immediate contact with the inmates, because in the course of the years the guard personnel had deteriorated to such an extent that the former standards could no longer be maintained...

"We had thousands of guards who could hardly speak German, who came from all leading countries of the world as volunteers and joined these units; or we had elder men, between 50 and 60, who lacked all interest in their work, so that a camp commandant had to take care continuously that these men fulfilled even the lowest requirements of their duties.

"Furthermore, it is obvious that there were elements among them who would ill-treat detainees, but this ill-treatment was never tolerated.

"Furthermore, it was impossible to have these masses of people working or when in the camp directed by SS men, so that everywhere detainees had to be engaged to give instructions to the detainees and set them to work, and who almost exclusively had the administration of the inner camp in their hands. Of course, a great deal of ill-treatment occurred which couldn't be avoided, because at night there was hardly any member of the SS in the camps. Only in specific cases were the SS men allowed to enter the camp, so that the detainees were more or less exposed to the detainee supervisors."

Question (by defense attorney for the SS, Dr. Babel):

"You have already mentioned regulations which existed for the guards, but there was also a standing order in all the camps. In this camp order there were laid down the punishments for detainees who violated the camp rules. What punishments were these?"

Answer:

"First of all, transfer to a 'penal company' (Strafkompanie), that is to say, harder work, and their accommodation restricted; next, detention in the cell block, detention in a dark cell; and in very serious cases, chaining or strapping. Punishment by 'strapping' (Anbinden) was prohibited in the year 1942 or 1943, I can't say exactly when, by the Reichsführer. Then there was the punishment of standing to attention during a long period at the entrance to the camp (Strafstehen), and finally punishment by beating.

"However, this punishment of beating could not be decreed by any commandant independently. He could apply for it."

Oral testimony of Rudolf Höss, 15 April 1946 (XI 403-411 [445-454]).

Höss's motivation appears to have been to protect his wife and 3 children, and to save the lives of others by testifying that only 60 people knew of the mass killings. Höss attempted to save Kaltenbrunner by implicating Eichmann and Pohl, who had not yet been apprehended. (For a similar case, see Heisig's affidavit implicating Raeder, XIII 460-461 [509-510]).

Höss appeared as a "defense witness", and his cross-examination by the prosecution was cut short by the prosecution itself (XI 418-419 [461-462]). Perhaps they were afraid he would spill the beans.

Höss's famous "autobiography" *Kommandant in Auschwitz*, probably prepared in question and answer from through interrogation like a gigantic "affidavit", then written up to be copied in his handwriting, is not much better. In this book, German text, cremation fires were visible for miles (p. 159), the stink was perceptible for miles (p. 179). Everyone in the area knew of the exterminations (p. 159), the victims knew they were going to be gassed (pp. 110, 111, 125), but it was possible to fool them (pp. 123-124; Document 3868-PS), and his family never knew a thing (pp. 129-130). Höss was a chronic drunkard who "confessed" these things when he had been drinking (p. 95) or was being tortured (p. 145).

It is not true that, according to p. 126 of this text, bodies were removed from gas chambers by Kapos eating and smoking and/or not wearing gas masks; the text does not say that. Dr Robert Faurisson has proven that Höss did make this assertion, but elsewhere, during an "interrogation". The Polish "translation" of this book, published prior to the publication of the German "original text", seems to agree with the German text, except that place names and dates are missing, indicating that the Polish was probably written first, these details being inserted later in the German translation. The uncut, unexpurgated complete writings of Rudolf Höss (?) (in Polish) are available through international library loan (*Wspomnienia Rudolfa Hössa, Komendanta Obozu Oswiecimskiego*).

JAPANESE WAR CRIMES TRIALS

While Germans were being convicted of making human "soap" (taken seriously in the seventh edition of Oppenheim and Lauterpacht's prestigious *International Law*, vol. II, p. 450) Japanese defendants were being convicted of making human "soup" in repeated trials.

This is not a misprint; it was considered a "proven fact" in 1948 – a "fact" proven in numerous "trials" – that the Japanese are a race of habitual cannibals who were forbidden upon pain of death from devouring the corpses of their own dead, but who were officially encouraged to eat Americans. Americans were served fried, or as soup; people were eaten when other food was available. Thus, the Japanese engage in cannibalism out of choice rather than necessity.

General Yamashita

Favourite human body parts for culinary purposes are liver, pancreas and gall bladder; Chinese are swallowed in pill form! Among the "trials" in which this was "proven" are:

- U.S. v Tachibana Yochio and 13 others, Mariana Islands, 2nd-15th August, 1946;
- Commonwealth of Australia vs. Tazaki Takehiko, Wewak, 30th November 1945;
- Commonwealth of Australia v. Tomiyasu Tisato, Rabaul, 2nd April 1946; and
- the most complex war crimes trial in history, the International Military Tribunal for the Far East (IMTFE) personally supervised by Douglas McArthur, which lasted from May 1946 until December 1948 (see *The Tokyo Judgment*, vol. 1, pp. 409-410, University of Amsterdam Press 1977, pp. 49,674-5 of mimeographed transcript).

The 25 defendants who survived trial were all convicted; 7 were hanged. Their crimes included:

- planning, initiation and waging "aggressive war" against the

Soviet Union (the Soviet Union attacked Japan two days after Hiroshima in violation of a Non-Aggression Pact; on this same day the London Agreement was signed, pursuant to which the Nuremberg Trial was held);
- planning, initiation, and waging "aggressive war" against France (France is in Europe);
- illegal sea blockade and indiscriminate population bombing (case against Shimada), that is, the actions of the British in Europe would have been illegal if committed by the Japanese;
- trial of war criminals before a military tribunal (case against Hata and Tojo; see also U.S. vs. Sawada, probably the most disgusting and hypocritical accusation of all; the victims were 7 Americans guilty of participating in the fire-bombing of Tokyo in which 80,000 women and children were burned to death); and
- cannibalism. It was not alleged that the defendants ate anyone personally.

The evidence included:
- Soviet War Crimes Reports
- Chinese War Crimes Reports
- Soviet reports based on Japanese documents not attached to the reports
- Summaries of Japanese military aggression in China (written by the Chinese)
- 317 Judge Advocate General War Crimes Reports (total length: 14,618 pages) "quoting" "captured" Japanese documents, diaries, cannibalism confessions, mass murder orders, orders to gas POWs on remote South Sea islands, etc. ("captured documents" not attached to reports; proof of authenticity or existence not required)
- affidavits of Japanese soldiers imprisoned in Siberia
- affidavits of Japanese referring to Japs as the "enemy"
- affidavits of Red Army Officers
- affidavits of illiterate natives on South Sea islands
- newspaper clippings (admissible evidence for the prosecution, but not usually for the defense); i.e., events in China were proven by quoting the *Chicago Daily Tribune*, the *New Orleans Times-Picayune*, the *Sacrimento Herald*, *Oakland Tribune*, *New York Herald*, *New York Times*, *Christian Science Monitor*, etc.
- the "affidavit" of Marquis Takugawa (written in English and not read to him in Japanese)
- the statements of Okawa (Okawa was declared insane and con-

fined to a lunatic asylum, but his statements were used in evidence)
- the testimony of Tanaka (a professional witness paid by the Americans; Okawa, when drunk, has confessed everything to Tanaka; Tanaka "The Monster" Ryukichi was supposedly responsible for millions of atrocities but was not tried, instead he moved freely about Japan)
- Kido's diary (titbits of gossip about everybody Kido did not like)
- Harada's Memoirs (Harada had suffered a stroke, so his dictation was incomprehensible; how well he could remember and what he meant to say were anybody's guess; the translations were a guess; many different "copies" had been "corrected" by a variety of people other than the person to whom he had dictated; added to which he had a reputation for telling lies).

The Prosecution's Answer to Defense Arguments at the end of the trial refutes all defensive evidence, stating that documents (translations of excerpts "copies" without proof of issuance or signature) are the best witnesses. If prosecution and defense both quote a document, defense have quoted out of context, but never the prosecution. Hearsay has probative value; testimony of defense witnesses has no probative value; cross-examination is a waste of time.

Five of the 11 judges – William Webb of Australia, Delfin Jaranilla of the Philippines, and Bert. A. Röling of the Netherlands, Henri Bernhard of France, and R.B. Pal of India – dissented.

Pal wrote a famous 700 page dissentient opinion in which he called the prosecution atrocity evidence "mostly worthless", remarking sarcastically that he hoped one of the documents was in Japanese.

A peculiarity of war crimes trials is that far from "proving" anything, they all contradict each other. It was held at Tokyo that the Chinese had a "right" to violate "unfair" treaties, and that Japanese efforts to enforce such treaties – because they were "unfair" – constituted "aggression".

When the atomic bombs were dropped, Shigemitsu had been attempting to negotiate a surrender for nearly 11 months, beginning on September 14, 1944. This of course became another "crime" – "prolonging the war through negotiation".

"Proof" of Japanese cannibal activity may be found in JAG Report 317, pp. 12,467-8 of mimeographed transcript; Exhibits 1446 and 1447, pp. 12,576-7; Exhibit 1873, pp. 14,129-30, and Exhibits 2056 and 2056A and B, pp. 15,032-42.

ALFRED JODL

Jodl was hanged for complicity in the Commando Order, an order to shoot British soldiers who fought in civilian clothes and strangled their own prisoners of war (XV 316-329 [347-362]).

Jodl's defense was that international law is intended to protect men who fight as soldiers. Soldiers are required to bear arms openly, wear clearly recognizable emblems or uniforms, and to treat prisoners in a humane manner.

Partisan warfare and the activities of British commando units were prohibited. Trial and execution of such people is legal if carried out under the terms of Article 63 of the Geneva Prisoner of War Convention of 1929.

(See also dissentient opinion of Judge Rutledge, U.S. v. Yamashita; Habeas Corpus action of Field Marshall Milch.)

In fact, almost no one was shot as a result of the Commando Order (55 in Western Europe, according to Sir David Maxwell-Fyfe, XXII 284 [325]).

The intention was to deter men from fighting in this manner, thinking they could simply surrender afterwards. Another "crime" was notifying the Commander in Chief of the Army that Hitler had repeated an already previously issued order that an offer of surrender from Leningrad was not to be accepted.

Like so many German crimes, this remained an idea without effect, since no offer of surrender ever came. The intention was to force the population to withdraw to the rear, since it would be impossible to feed millions of people or to prevent epidemics. Gaps were left in German lines to the East in order to enable the population to do this. Kiev, Odessa, and Kharkov had capitulated but were mined, killing thousands of German soldiers with delayed-action detonator devices. The docks were required for military purposes; Russian railroads were on a different gauge from German ones, and supplies could not be brought forward to feed millions of half-starved prisoners or Jews. The Soviet propaganda lie that Germans killed millions of Russian prisoners has been taken seriously by many people who do not know the causes of the mortality.

The order concerning Leningrad, Document C-123, is not signed.

The case against Jodl illustrates the absurdity of the entire trial. In the words of his defense attorney, Dr. Exner:

"Murder and revolution – in peacetime this would have meant civil war; in wartime, the immediate collapse of the front and the end of the Reich. Should he then have cried, 'Fiat justia, pereat patria?'

"It really appears that the prosecution holds the view that such conduct could be demanded of the defendants. An astonishing idea! Whether murder and treason can ever be justified ethically had better be left to moralists and theologians. At all events, jurists cannot even discuss such an idea. To be obliged on pain of punishment to murder the head of state? A soldier should do that? And in wartime? Those who have committed such deeds have always been punished, but to punish them for not doing so would indeed be something new." (XIX 45 [54]; XXII 86-90 [100-105]).

At Tokyo, the generals were hanged for interfering in politics.

At another point, Dr. Exner exclaimed, "On one single page of the Anglo-American trial brief the phrase 'Jodl was present at' occurs six times. What does this mean legally?" (XIX 37 [44]).

Jodl was asked by one of the Soviet prosecutors, Col. Pokrovsky, "Do you know that the German troops... quartered, hanged upside down, and roasted Soviet captives over the fire? Did you know that?"

To which Jodl replied, "Not only did I not know it, but I do not even believe it" (XV 545 [595]).

This is the entire vast subject of war crimes trials boiled down into 3 sentences (XV 284-561 [313-612]; XVIII 506-510 [554-558]; XIX 1-46 [7-55]).

ERNST KALTENBRUNNER

During Kaltenbrunner's cross examination, he was indignantly asked how he had the nerve to pretend he was telling the truth and that 20 or 30 witnesses were lying (XI 349 [385]).

The "eyewitnesses", of course, did not appear in court; they were merely names on pieces of paper. One of these names is that of Franz Ziereis, commandant of Mauthausen concentration camp.

Ziereis "confessed" to gassing 65,000 people; making lamp-shades out of human skin; manufacturing counterfeit money; and supplied a complicated table of statistical information containing the exact number of inmates in 31 different camps.

He then accused Kaltenbrunner of ordering the entire camp (Mauthausen) to be killed upon the approach of the Americans.

Ziereis had been dead for 10 and a half months when he made this "confession". Fortunately, the "confession" has been "remembered" by someone else: a concentration camp inmate named Hans Marsalek, who never appeared in court, but whose signature appears on the document (Document 3870-PS, XXXIII 279-286).

Pages 1 through 6 of this document are in quotation marks (!), including the statistical table, which states, for example, that there were 12,000 inmates at Ebensee; 12,000 at Mauthausen; 24,000 at Gusen I and II; 20 inmates at Schloss-Lindt, 70 inmates at Klagenfurt-Junkerschule, etc, for all of 31 camps in the table.

The document is not signed by anyone else alleged to have been present at Ziereis's "confession", and no notes alleged to have been taken at the time are appended to the document. The document bears two signatures only: that of Hans Marsalek, the inmate; and that of Smith W. Brookhart Jr. U.S. Army.

The document bears the date 8 April 1946. Ziereis died 23 May 1945.

The pretense was that Ziereis was too seriously injured (he died of multiple gunshot wounds through the stomach) to sign anything at the time, but he was healthy enough to dictate this lengthy and complex document, which was then "remembered" exactly and verbatim by Marsalek for 10 and a half months. Marsalek would, of course, have had no motivation to lie.

The document is in German. Brookhart was a confession ghostwriter who also wrote the "confessions" of Rudolf Höss (in English, Document 3868-PS) and Otto Ohlendorf (in German, Document 2620-PS).

(Brookhart was the son of a Senator from Washington Iowa. Address in 1992: 18 Hillside Drive, Denver Colorado, USA. Brookhart never answered my letter as to whether he had any papers or memoirs.)

Ziereis' "confession" continues to be taken seriously by Reitlinger, Shirer, Hilberg, and other itinerant peddlers of Holo-Schlock.

Kaltenbrunner claimed that there were 13 central concentration camps or "Stammlager" during the war (XI 268-269 [298-299]). The prosecution total of 300 concentration camps was achieved by including perfectly normal work camps.

The 13th camp, Matzgau, near Danzig, was a special camp whose prisoners were SS guards and police who had been sentenced to imprisonment for offenses against prisoners in their charge: physical mistreatment, embezzlement, theft of personal property, etc.

This camp with its inmate SS men fell into the hands of the Russians at the end of the war (XI 312, 316 [345, 350]).

Kaltenbrunner claimed that sentences passed by SS and police courts were far more severe than sentences passed by other courts for the same offenses.

The SS carried out frequent trials of their own men for offenses against inmates and violations of discipline (XXI 264-291, 369-370 [294-323, 408-409]).

Third degree methods of interrogation were permitted by law for the sole purpose of obtaining information relating to future resistance activity; it was forbidden for the purpose of obtaining confessions. These interrogators required the presence of a doctor, and allowed a total of 20 blows with a stick once only, on the bare buttocks, a process which could not be repeated later. Other forms of legal "Nazi torture" included confinement in a dark cell, or standing during lengthy interrogations (XX 164, 180-181 [184, 202-203]; XXI 502-510; 528-530 [556-565, 583-584]).

Kaltenbrunner and many other defense witnesses claimed that similar methods were used by police all over the world (XI 312 [346]) and that respected police officials visited Germany to study German procedures (XXI 373 [412]).

Defense evidence on this and related topics amounts to many thousands of pages divided between the Tribunal and "commission", and 136,000 affidavits (XXI 346-373 [382-412]; 415 [458], 444 [492]).

Kaltenbrunner was convicted of conspiring to "lynch" Allied airmen who committed mass bombings of civilians. The lynchings would have been illegal, but did not occur. Many airmen were saved from mobs by German officials. The Germans refused to contemplate such a matter, fearing it would lead to a general slaughter of parachuted fliers. Like so many other German crimes, this remained an idea without effect (XXI 406-407 [449-450], 472-476 [522-527]).

Another crime committed by Kaltenbrunner was responsibility for the so-called "Bullet Order". This is supposed to have been an order to shoot prisoners of war using a measuring contraption (probably inspired by the Paul Waldmann pedal-driven brain bashing machine, Document USSR-52, VII 377 [416-417]).

The "Bullet Order", Document 1650-PS, if it is an authentic document, which it probably is not (XVIII 35-36 [43-44]) is a mistranslation: the sense of the order is that prisoners who attempt to escape should be chained to an iron ball (Kugel), and not that they should be shot with a "bullet" (also Kugel). The word "chained" appears in the document, but the word "shot" does not (III 506 [565]; XXI 514 [568]; Gestapo affidavit 75; XXI 299 [332]). The document is a "teletype" thus, without a signature (XXVII 424-428).

"Sonderbehandlung" (special treatment) is an example of the ugly jargon used in all bureaucracies, and is probably best translated as "treatment on a case by case basis".

Kaltenbrunner was able to show that it meant, in the context of one document, the right to drink champagne and take French lessons. The prosecution got a winter resort mixed up with a concentration camp (XI 338-339 [374-375]) (XI 232-386 [259-427]; XVIII 40-68 [49-80]). (The winter resort document is Document 3839-PS, XXXIII 197-199, an "affidavit".)

WILHELM KEITEL

Keitel was hanged for alleged responsibility in atrocities said to have been committed in Russia, and for the Commissar and Night and Fog Decrees.

The evidence against Keitel consists largely of the "reports" of Soviet War Crimes Commissions (XVII 611-612 [663-664], XXII 76-83 [90-98]). These are summaries containing final judgments, conclusions, and generalizations without any underlying evidence or documents. In these reports, military agencies are wrongly named and confused.

Among the Soviet documents used to convict Keitel are Documents USSR-4; 9; 10; 35; 38; 40; 90; 364; 366; 407; and 470.

USSR-4 is a "report" which alleges intentional spreading of typhus epidemics to exterminate the Russian population. Responsibility for this crime is attributed to the "Hitler Government and the Supreme Command of the Armed Forces"; see also *Report on U.S. Crimes in Korea*, Peking (1952) (American Germ Warfare).

Documents USSR-9, 35, and 38 are also Soviet War Crimes Reports.

Document USSR-90 is the judgment of a Soviet military court, and states that "German fascist intruders committed bestial crimes", and attributes these crimes to the "German Armed Forces Command".

Original documents are not appended, and specific orders are not mentioned. Keitel's name is not mentioned. The other documents are "certified true copies" (XVIII 9-12 [16-19]) of documents supposedly possessed by the Russians.

The "Night and Fog Decree" (XVIII 19-22 [27-30]) was intended as an alternative to shooting resistance members. It was conceded by the prosecution that such people could be legally shot (V 405 [456]) but the Germans considered it undesirable to sentence everyone to death. Prison sentences were felt to have little deterrent value, since everyone expected the war to end in a few years (XXI 524 [578-579]).

The Commissar Order had little if any practical effect, partly due to the difficulty of determining who was a Commissar (XXI 404-405 [446-447]; XXII 77 [91]). Keitel is accused to this day of blocking access to Hitler, that is, shielding Hitler from certain information. This accusation, absurd in the extreme, is refuted on pages 645-661 [710-717] of volume XVII.

Also used against Keitel was Document 81-PS, quoted in Jackson's opening speech, and Document USSR-470, a "true copy" (meaning the document has been re-typed to make the copy) of an "original document" written entirely in Serbo-Croat, and supposedly located in Yugoslavia, with a typewritten signature by Keitel. It was not alleged that Keitel understood Serbo-Croat, rather that this was a "translation" of a document written in German which the Yugoslavians did not find (XV 530-536 [578-585]).

Keitel's case appears at X 468-658 [527-724]; XI 1-28 [7-37]; XVII 603-661 [654-717]; XVIII 1-40 [7-48].

CONSTANTIN VON NEURATH

Von Neurath was the victim of a major forgery, Document 3859-PS. The Czechs re-typed an authentic document, making extensive alterations and additions, and presented a "photocopy" of their "copy" (with typewritten signatures) to the Tribunal. The original document was in Czechoslovakia.

On this document, nearly everything is wrong: German bureaucracy was extremely complex, and many prosecution documents bear wrong addresses, false references, and incorrect procedural markings which are not immediately obvious. In relation to this document, Von Neurath said, "I regret to say that you are lying" (XVII 67 [79]; 373-377 [409-413]).

Von Neurath was convicted of closing Czech universities (not a crime under international law when performed by an occupation government) and shooting 9 Czech student leaders after a demonstration. These crimes were "proven" with various documents:

USSR-489, a "certified true copy", certified by the Czechs;

USSR-60, a "report" of a "War Crimes Commission", quoting the "statements" of Karl Hermann Frank, which were not appended to the report; and USSR-494, an "affidavit" signed by Karl Hermann Frank 33 days before his execution. The statements attributed to Frank in the War Crimes Report were, of course, not signed or dated, and the original documents were in Czechoslovakia (XVII 85-90 [98-104]).

Much of the "evidence" concocted against Von Neurath, Schacht, Von Papen, Raeder, and others came from the affidavits of an elderly American diplomat living in Mexico (Documents 1760-PS; 2385-PS; 2386-PS; EC-451).

The diplomat, Messersmith, was claimed to be too old to come to court (II 350 [387]); it was denied, however, that he was senile (II 352

[389]). The "evidence" consists of Messersmith's personal opinions as to the motivations and character of other people. Von Neurath's case appears at XVI 593-673 [649-737]; XVII 2-107 [9-121]; XIX 216-311 [242-345].

FRANZ VON PAPEN

Von Papen was accused of conspiring with Hitler to induce Hindenburg to take Hitler into government as Reichschancellor. According to this view, Hindenburg was deceived by Von Papen into believing that civil war would ensue if this was not done.

The Reichschancellor at that time, General Von Schleicher, had attempted to rule illegally and unconstitutionally for some time without the support of the National Socialists, who enjoyed the largest majority in the history of the Reichstag. Many of Hitler's illegalities actually date back to the period of Von Schleicher's rule (XXII 102-103 [118-119]). This was the only alternative to the chaos of 41 political parties, each representing some private financial interest.

The democratic victors demanded of Von Papen, in 1946, that he should have foreseen Hitler's intent to wage "aggressive war" in 1933, and conspired with Von Schleicher to rule through military dictatorship.

Von Schleicher was later shot following the Rohm Putsch. These shootings were considered legal by Hindenburg, as was evidenced by a telegram congratulating Hitler (XX 291 [319]; XXI 350 [386]; 577-578 [636-637]; XXII 117 [134-135]).

Von Papen also considered the shooting of Rohm and his followers to have been justified by emergency (XVI 364 [401]), but considered that many other murders took place which were not justified, and that it was Hitler's duty to conduct an investigation and punish these acts. This was not done.

It was conceded by the prosecution at Nuremberg that the Nazi Party Program contained nothing illegal, and was indeed almost laudable (II 105 [123]). The National Socialists were declared legal by the occupation authorities in the Rheinland in 1925 (XXI 455 [505]) and by the

German Supreme Court in 1932 (XXI 568 [626]) and by the League of Nations and Polish Resident General in Danzig in 1930 (XVIII 169 [187-188]).

It was not clear in 1933 that the Army would unanimously support Von Schleicher against the National Socialists, who had a legal right to govern.

Hindenburg's refusal to violate the Constitution at the risk of civil war brought Hitler into government in an entirely legal manner (see also XXII 111-112 [128-129]).

Von Papen was accused of "immoral acts in furtherance of the Common Plan", such as the use of the intimate "du" form in conversation with the Austrian Foreign Minister, Guido Schmidt: Von Papen remarked, "Sir David, if you had ever been in Austria in your life, you would know that in Austria almost everyone says 'du' to everyone else" (XVI 394 [435]).

Acts of Von Papen's which could not be called "criminal" were used to prove the defendant's "duplicity" (no pun intended). A mental construction was placed on Von Papen's acts with the benefit of hindsight.

It is sometimes alleged that since Von Papen, Fritzsche and Schacht were acquitted, Nuremberg was a "fair trial". The contrary does not apply to the International Military Tribunal of the Far East, or other trials in which there were no acquittals; it is forgotten that the witchcraft trials of the 17th Century averaged 5-10% in acquittals. Von Papen's case appears at XVI 236-422 [261-466]; XIX 124-177 [139-199].

ERICH RAEDER

Raeder was accused of "conspiring" with the Japanese to attack the United States.

Other crimes committed by Raeder included listening to speeches, being present at conferences, having knowledge of contingency plans, and accepting birthday gifts.

Raeder proved that the Americans knew of the impending Pearl Harbour attack 10 days before it occurred, while the Germans knew nothing (XIV 122 [137-138]).

Raeder's discussion of German military preparedness and Hitler speeches will be discussed together with Von Ribbentrop's (XIII 595-599 [656-660]; 617-631 [680-696]; XIV 1-246 [7-275]; XVIII 372-430 [406-470]).

JOACHIM VON RIBBENTROP

Von Ribbentrop was hanged for signing the Molotov-Ribbentrop Pact, which preceded and made possible the attack on Poland. Ribbentrop defended his actions on the grounds that one million Germans had been expelled from Polish territory over a 20-year period, accompanied by numerous atrocities, and that complaints to the World Court in The Hague and the League of Nations in Geneva had been ignored for just as long. These were ethnic Germans with Polish citizenship living in lands given to the new Polish state under the Versailles Treaty.

On October 23, 1938, Ribbentrop made an offer to the Poles which the British ambassador, Sir Neville Henderson, admitted was reasonable, calling it a "pure League of Nations proposal": Ribbentrop asked for a plebiscite in the Polish corridor; the return of Danzig (a 100% German city) to the Reich, and the construction of an extra-territorial double-track railway and highway across the Corridor to East Prussia, which had previously been separated from the rest of Germany and could only be reached by sea, in defiance of all common sense, that is, a land bridge to East Prussia (X 260-269 [295-304]; 280-281 [317-318]; 367-369 [416-417]).

In return, the Poles were to receive an advantageous financial settlement: a guarantee of port facilities and outlet for Polish goods through the port of Danzig. The future of the Corridor was to be decided according to the principle of self-determination, the Poles would receive an outlet to the sea, and the German-Polish Friendship Pact (signed by Hitler in 1934 in the face of bitter German opposition), would be renewed for an additional period (XIX 362-368 [399-406]).

(For the prosecution version of these same events, see III 209-229 [237-260].)

This was the "Nazi Plan to conquer the world" which served as a pretext for the entire war, including, eventually, Pearl Harbor, Hiroshima, and Yalta.

In reply, the Poles maintained that any change in the status of Danzig would mean war with Poland. A general mobilization was ordered. The expulsions continued, filling refugee camps along the Polish border.

The Polish ambassador, Lipski, reportedly stated on August 31, 1939, that he was well aware of conditions in Germany, having served there for many years. He was not interested in any note or proposal from Germany. In the event of war, revolution would break out in Germany, and the Polish Army would march in triumph to Berlin (XVII 520-521 [565-566]; 564-566 [611-614]; XX 607 [661]).

Ribbentrop claimed that the attitude of the Poles made war inevitable; that the problem of the Corridor and the expulsions had to be solved; that for both Hitler and Stalin the territories involved had been lost to both countries after a disastrous war followed by equally disastrous treaties (X 224-444 [254-500]; XVII 555-603 [602-655]).

To the Germans at Nuremberg, there appeared only one explanation: the Poles and the British were in contact with the so-called German underground, which had grossly exaggerated its own importance (XVII 645-661 [699-717]; XIII 111-112 [125-126]).

Hitler's interpreter appeared as a witness, and testified that the Germans could not believe that the British would go to war over something which their ambassador admitted was reasonable. According to the interpreter, Paul Schmidt, there was a full minute of silence when the message of the British declaration of war was delivered, after which Hitler turned to Ribbentrop and said "What shall we do now?" (X 200 [227]).

Schmidt's testimony shed light on a famous remark attributed to Von Ribbentrop, that Jews should be killed or confined to concentration camps.

What happened, according to Schmidt (X 203-204 [231]) was that Hitler was putting pressure on Horthy to take stronger measures against Jews. Horthy said, "What am I supposed to do? I can't kill them." Ribbentrop was very irritable and said, "There are two alternatives: either you can do just that, or they can be interned."

This appeared in the minutes of the conference as "The Reichs Foreign Minister said that Jews should be killed or confined to concentration camps". The statement was used against Ribbentrop and all other defendants during the trial, despite Schmidt's testimony that the minutes were inaccurate (X 410-411 [462-463]).

According to Ribbentrop, Raeder, Göring, and nearly all defendants except Schacht, the Germans were not prepared for war and did not plan "aggression" (XVII 522 [566-567]; XXII 62, 90 [76, 105]).

The invasion of Belgium, Holland, and France were not "aggression", because France had declared war on Germany. Belgium and Holland allowed British planes to fly over their countries every night to bomb the Ruhr. The Germans protested in writing 127 times (XVII 581 [630], XIX 10 [16]).

Göring, Raeder, Milch and many others testified that Germany had only 26 Atlantic submarines with insufficient torpedoes, as opposed to 315 submarines in 1919 (XIV 26 [34]), and a "ridiculous" bomb supply (XIX 4-5 [11-12]).

Hitler told Field Marshall Milch in May 1939 that there was no need for full bomb production, as there would be no war. Milch replied that full bomb production would take several months to bring to capacity. The order to begin full production of bombs was not given until October 12 or 20, 1939 (IX 50 [60-61]; XVII 522 [566-567]).

The German Air Force was designed for defensive, pin-point bombing; the Germans cooperated with both the Russians and the British in exchange of technical information of military value until 1938 (IX 45-133 [54-153]; XIV 298-351 [332-389]).

The Germans never built anywhere near the number of ships and especially submarines (XIV 24 [31]) allowed to them under the terms of the Anglo-German Naval Accord of 1935 (XVIII 379-389 [412-425]). This agreement represented a recognition by the British that the Versailles Treaty was out of date. It was also a voluntarily undertaken limitation by Hitler of German naval armament (XIX 224-232 [250-259]).

When war broke out, many large German battleships were still under construction and had to be scrapped, because they would have taken years to finish (XIII 249-250 [279-280]; 620-624 [683-687]). According to an affidavit signed by her captain, one of Germany's largest battleships, the Gneisenau, was on a training cruise near the Canary Islands when war broke out, without any ammunition supplies (XXI 385 [425]).

Hitler was a bluffer who loved to terrify politicians with grossly illogical, self-contradictory speeches (XIV 34-48 [43-59]; 329-330 [366]), which all contradicted each other (XXII 66-68 [80-81]). For this reason, exact stenographic notes were never taken until 1941 (XIV 314-315 [349-350]).

Many "Hitler speeches" are semi-falsifications or forgeries (XVII 406-408 [445-447], XVIII 390-402 [426-439]; XXII 65 [78-79]).

The Germans believed they were no longer bound by the Versailles Treaty because its terms – the preamble to Part V – had been violated by the British, and especially the French. German disarmament was to be followed by general disarmament (IX 4-7 [12-14]; XIX 242 [269], 356 [392]).

Hitler had offered to disarm to the last machine gun, provided other nations did likewise; but Germany could not remain in a weakened position forever, to be invaded and crushed at any moment. The reoccupation of the Rhineland gave Germany a natural frontier protecting the Ruhr, and would have been a matter of course for any government. Eastern Europe seethed with conflict between heavily armed states; East Prussia was not defensible; the Poles were openly demanding parts of Upper Silesia (XII 476-479 [520-524]; XIX 224-232 [249-259], XX 570-571 [623-624]).

The French-Soviet Accord of 5 December 1934 violated the Locarno Pact, which the Germans were convicted of violating (XIX 254, 269, 277 [283, 299, 308]). It was not clear that the occupation of the remainder of Czechoslovakia violated the Munich Accord (X 259 [293-294]). This was done because the Russians were building airports there, in cooperation with the Czechs. The Czechs hoped to turn the remainder of Czechoslovakia into a "aircraft carrier" from which Germany could be attacked (X 348 [394-395]; 427-430 [480-484]).

Roosevelt had declared that American interest extended to all of the Western Hemisphere, and Britain claimed dominion over half the world; surely German interest could extend as far as Czechoslovakia. From Prague to Berlin by plane is half an hour; Czech actions were plainly threatening to German security.

There is no such thing as a treaty which lasts forever. Generally, they are superceded by subsequent treaties, and become obsolete. This is usually covered in the language of the treaty itself by the words "rebus sic stantibus". By 1935, Versailles and Lucarno had become obsolete.

ALFRED ROSENBERG AND ERNST SAUCKEL

Like Frank, Rosenberg was accused of "looting" and "plundering" works of art.

Rosenberg and Frank both pointed out that Germany was required to protect works of art under the terms of The Hague Convention, and that doing so required removing them from the scene of hostilities. The artworks were carefully packed, appraised and repaired. Had it been the German intention to "loot" or to "steal", it would not have been necessary to catalogue these artworks with an exact notation of the name and address of the owner, if that was known.

Several works of art were appropriated by Göring, not for Göring's personal use, but for a museum which Hitler intended to create in Linz.

Rosenberg protested against this appropriation on the grounds that it was his duty to maintain the collections intact until the end of the war in the hope that a peace settlement could be made regarding these objects.

Rosenberg was also accused of stealing thousands of railroad car loads of furniture. The furniture had belonged to Jews who had abandoned their homes upon German arrival in Paris. The Jewish apartments were sealed for 90 days, then the property in them was confiscated as abandoned, since its safekeeping could not be assured. Eventually it was used for the benefit of Germans who had been rendered homeless by bombing raids. Again, it was hoped to make a settlement at the end of the war.

Rosenberg's ministry received a large number of complaints, which were investigated. many were found to have no basis in fact. At Nuremberg, it was simply assumed that every complaint was "true". Letters to Rosenberg were used against him in evidence, though his answers to those letters had been lost. The complaints and letters were held to prove "willing membership in the Common Plan".

Rosenberg was accused of conspiring with Sauckel to obtain "slaves" for the war effort from the occupied territories. Rosenberg, Sauckel, Speer, Göring, and Seyss-Inquart all protested that had it not been for the Allied blockade such "plundering" and "slavery" would not have been necessary; that the sea blockade was illegal, and caused mass unemployment in the occupied territories; and that occupation governments are allowed to demand payment in services under the Hague Convention. The "slaves" were paid the same wages as  German workers, who were also subject to compulsory labour. Funk claimed the "slaves" remitted 2 billion Reichsmarks in wages to their families (XIII 136 [153]). Seyss-Inquart claimed there were 500,000 unemployed in Holland as a result of the blockade, and if they were not provided with employment, voluntary or otherwise, they would join the resistance movement, illegal under international law. They were quite happy to work on German fortifications in Holland, because this made it less likely that the Allied invasion would take place in Holland.

(The likelihood of Allied invasion was also the reason for the deportation of Dutch Jews) (XV 662-668 [719-726]; XIX 99-102 [113-115]).

Fritzsche and others testified that the "slaves" could be seen moving about freely in all German cities (XVII 163-164 [183-184]), had plenty of money, and controlled the black market (XIV 590 [649]). Moreover, hundreds of thousands of these "slaves" refused to leave the country after the war, even though their own countries had been "liberated" and Germany was devastated (XVIII 155 [172-173]).

Nor did the "slaves" revolt at the end of the war (XVIII 129-163 [144-181]; 466-506 [509-554]; XIX 177-216 [199-242]; XXI 471-472 [521-522]).

Sauckel testified that the "slave labour" recruitment in France was carried out by the French government and by French collaborationist organizations. Many persons wished to be "compelled" in order to avoid reprisals by the resistance (XV 1-263 [7-290]) but all were paid the same wages as German workers and enjoyed the same health benefits and terms of contract.

Far from "looting" the occupied territories, it was necessary to import much valuable equipment. In Russia, everything had been destroyed during the retreat by the Russians. When Germans imported equipment and withdrew it during their own retreat, this was called "looting" (IX 171-172 [195-196]).

An example of a "complaint" which became a "crime" was the case in which theatre goers were reportedly rounded up into "slavery". Sauckel investigated for some months, and found this to have been a case in which a labour contractor interrupted a party of his own workers in order to move them to another workplace (XV 17-18 [25-26]).

As conditions worsened, more compulsion became necessary. If the Allies had the right to confiscate property of neutrals at sea, the Germans had the right to utilize the resources of occupied territories on land.

Another accusation against Rosenberg was the so-called "Hay Action", in which 50,000 children were "kidnapped" into "slave labour". Rosenberg and Von Schirach both testified that this was an apprenticeship program designed to remove orphans from the war zone (XI 489-490 [538-539] XIV 501-505 [552-556]).

If Rosenberg's ministry did not remove the orphans from the area, the Army would do it.

A related accusation is the "Lebensborn" organization, supposedly a plot to kidnap babies after measuring the size of their penises (according to mentally ill Jewish "historians"). The purpose of this organization was to remove the stigma of illegitimacy and to aid families with numerous children (XXI 654-664, German volumes. These pages have disappeared from the American transcript. See also XXI 352 [389]).

(Rosenberg's case appears at XI 444-599 [490-656]; XVIII 69-128 [81-143]).

HJALMAR SCHACHT

Schacht is an anomaly as a defendant because the accusations against him contradict those made against the other defendants. While the others were accused of "acts of moral turpitude" proving their "willing membership or participation in the conspiracy or Common Plan", such as accepting birthday gifts; making birthday speeches; being photographed; signing laws legally passed by the Head of State; being in political agreement with the Head of State; or if not, failing in their moral duty to overthrow and murder the Head of State (obviously not a duty that can be imposed by law); Schacht was accused of all these things, and, for good measure, violating his oath of loyalty to Hitler and deceiving Hitler! This was considered proof of particular wickedness (XII 597 [652-653]).

Schacht's remark on the necessity of lying has been widely quoted to prove Nazi duplicity; it is forgotten that the person being lied to was Hitler.

Schacht ridiculed these accusations with one wisecrack after another, and was even more sarcastic than Göring. Jackson, however, lacked the perspicacity to realize that Schacht was making a fool of him (XII 416-493 [454-539]; 507-602 [554-658]; XIII 1-48 [7-58]; XVIII 270-312 [299-342]).

Jackson's lie that he forced Schacht to "admit that he lied" has been taken seriously by many people who should know better. Jackson habitually lied (for example, II 438 [483]; IX 500-504 [555-559]).

BALDUR VON SCHIRACH

Von Schirach was accused of conspiring with millions of children to conquer the world in imitation Boy Scout uniforms. It was pointed out in his defense that a conspiracy involving millions of members is a logical absurdity (XIV 360-537 [399-592], XVIII 430-466 [470-509]).

To further this aim, the conspirators engaged in target practice with .22 calibre rifles (XIV 381 [420-421]) and sang songs which were sometimes 300 years old (XIV 474 [521]).

At Nuremberg, crimes could be found anywhere. In the case against the SA, an article on foot care was quoted to prove "intent to engage in aggressive war" (XXI 221-223 [248-250]).

Schirach was accused of knowledge of atrocities by Hans Marsalek, whose "recollection" of Ziereis's "confession" (6 pages in quotation marks) one year after Ziereis died, was used against Kaltenbrunner (XI 330-333 [365-369]; XIV 436-440 [480-485]).

Another crime committed by Schirach was being short and fat (affidavit of Georg Ziemer, 244-PS, XIV 400-401 [440-441]).

Schirach denied this charge. (A "short, fat student leader" had delivered an anti-Semitic speech.)

Schirach was supposed to have received Einsatzgruppen reports at his office as Gauleiter of Vienna. These documents are photocopies of "true copies" on plain paper without headings or signature, prepared by unknown persons, and found buried in a salt mine (II 157 [185]) by the Russians (IV 245 [273], VIII 293-301 [324-332]).

Katyn is listed as a German crime (NMT IV 112, Einsatzgruppen).

The Germans are supposed to have killed 22,000,000 people (XXII 238 [270]), or 12,000,000 (XXII 312 [356]), after which the bodies were burned and the documents were buried. Documents are combustible and bodies are not.

Schirach and Streicher were both taken in by a "photocopy" of a Hitler document in which he "confessed" to mass killings (XIV 432 [476]; XII 321 [349]).

Since Hitler was a genius (X 600 [671-672]), and since geniuses do not kill millions of people with Diesel exhaust and insecticides which take 24 hours to kill moths (Document NI-9912), it appears that the significance of this document has been overrated.

In fact, it is typical Hitler: full of violent language, but short of factual content. Nor is it certain that Hitler was of sound mind in 1945 (IX 92 [107]). The Hitler "confession" is a "certified" photocopy (Streicher Defense Document 9, XLI 547).

ARTHUR SEYSS-INQUART

Seyss-Inquart is an example of the manner in which perfectly legal actions were charged as "crimes" when undertaken by Germans, while identical actions, or actions criminal under the Tribunal's own Statute (such as the Dresden bombings, illegal under Article 6(b), XXII 471, 475 [535, 540]), were treated as the minor inconveniences of a great crusade to eradicate evil.

Under international law, occupation governments are allowed to legislate as they see fit (a right claimed by the Tribunal itself, XXII 461 [523], but contradicted at XXII 497 [565-566]) and obedience to their authority is required. They are allowed to conscript labour within certain limits, to confiscate government property, levy taxes to cover the costs of occupation, and are not required to tolerate armed resistance, striking, publication of hostile newspapers, or to employ local officials who will not follow orders.

Initialling documents or passing on orders are not crimes under international law. Seyss-Inquart prevented much unnecessary destruction at the end of the war which would have been illegal (XV 610-668 [664-726]; XVI 1-113 [7-128]; XIX 46-111 [55-125]).

As Reichskommissar for Holland, Seyss-Inquart passed on orders to execute resistance members after conviction for acts of sabotage or armed resistance, illegal under The Hague Convention. The executions were carried out after renewed acts of sabotage occurred. This was called "execution of hostages". The word "hostage", however, is incorrect (XII 95-96 [108], XVIII 17-19 [25-27], XXI 526 [581], 535 [590]).

For a discussion of international law from the prosecution point of view, conceding the legality of these actions, see V 537 [603-604]. It was conceded by the prosecution that resistance members may be shot (V 405 [455-456]).

The Fourth Hague Convention on Land Warfare of 18 October 1907 contains an all-participation clause (Art. 2); belligerents violating the convention may be required to pay compensation (Art. 3); prohibits bombardments "by whatever means" of undefended cities, cultural monuments (Art. 23). Not ratified by Bulgaria, Greece, Italy, Yugoslavia. Ratified by Czarist Russia.

ALBERT SPEER

Albert Speer was convicted of conspiring to enslave millions of people for work in German armaments industries, where they were forced to sleep in urinals (Document D-288, Affidavit of Dr. Wilhelm Jäger) and were tortured in mass-produced torture boxes disguised as clothes lockers (Document D-892), the bizarre "disguise" being intended to permit the introduction of perfectly ordinary objects as proof of "atrocities".

Regarding this charge, Speer said, "I consider this affidavit a lie... it is not possible to drag the German people in the dirt in such a way" (XVI 543 [594]).

Speer was the kind of man who is successful under any system. He always claimed he knew nothing about "exterminations", but said he would have heard about it if prisoners had been cremated using atomic bombs (a Robert Jackson hallucination, XVI 529-530 [580]).

Speer claimed to have plotted to assassinate Hitler using a highly sophisticated nerve gas (XVI 494-495 [542-544]). The plot failed because the gas could only be produced at high temperatures (XVI 529 [579]).

Actually, Zyklon-B presents a similar problem, in that the liquid must evaporate, and does so slowly unless heated. German technical wizardry and industrial advancement in general renders ridiculous any notion of a "Holocaust" using insecticide or Diesel exhaust. It would be more difficult to "drag the German people in the dirt" if it were not for people like Albert Speer. (XVI 430-588 [475-645]; XIX 177-216 [199-242].)

JULIUS STREICHER

Streicher was hanged for "incitement to race hatred", a crime which is becoming more popular. The Streicher case is remarkable in that nations which preach separation of church and state and freedom of speech and press should conspire with Jews and Communists to hang a man for expressing opinions which were not alleged to have been untrue.

One of Streicher's crimes was the publication of a "ritual murder" supplement in his anti-Semitic newspaper, *Der Stürmer*. It was expressly admitted by the prosecution that his illustrations were authentic (V 103 [119]) and that the article was referenced correctly.

Among Streicher's references was at least one recognised scholar, Dr. Erich Bischof of Leipzig, and modern legal proceedings (IX 696-700 [767-771]). It was felt that to investigate the validity of these references would have unduly prolonged the trial, so the article was not alleged to have been untrue.

Rather, an act of mental telepathy was performed, and Streicher was hanged for his alleged mental processes and motivation.

Another Streicher crime was calling the Old Testament "a horrible criminal romance... this 'holy book' abounds in murder, incest, fraud, theft and indecency". No evidence was introduced to rebut this view (V 96 [112]).

Streicher is famous as a "pornographer", "sex pervert" and "swindler". The "pornography collection", upon further examination, turned out to be the *Stürmer* archive of Judaica (XII 409 [445]). The "sex pervert" charge, heavily emphasized by the Russians, had as its origin the so-called Göring Report, a Party disciplinary proceeding brought by one of Streicher's many enemies. This charge was dropped at Nuremberg and stricken from the record; Streicher was told he need not answer any questions related to this accusation (XII 330, 339 [359, 369]).

The "property swindle" was also drawn from the Göring Report, and related to a single case, involving the Mars Works. The man responsible for the accusations contained in the report was, by some coincidence, the man responsible for the purchase (V 106 [123]). The report states that the shares were returned, and that the money that Streicher had paid for them, 5000 Reichsmarks, was returned to Streicher after the investigation.

Streicher gave his business managers full power of attorney to do as they liked, saying "Do not worry me with business matters There are other things more important than money". Streicher claimed his newspaper was published in a rented house until the end of the war. It was not a Party newspaper, and Streicher had nothing to do with the war.

One of Streicher's employees appeared as a witness and stated, "Whoever knows Herr Streicher as I do, knows that Herr Streicher has never taken anything from a Jew" (XII 385-386 [420]).

Streicher's second wife, Adele Streicher, appeared and stated, "I consider it quite impossible that Julius Streicher acquired shares that way. I believe that he does not even know what a share looks like" (XII 391 [426]).

It was not alleged at Nuremberg that Streicher wrote all his own articles and publications. "Trau keinem Fuchs auf gruner Heid, und keinem Jud' bei seinem Eid", translated by the prosecution as "Don't Trust a Fox Whatever You Do, Nor Yet the Oath of any Jew" (XXXVIII 129) took its title from Martin Luther.

"Der Giftpilz", (The Poisonous Fungus) was written by one of Streicher's editors, inspired by a famous child molester case, that of the Jewish industrialist, Louis Schloss (XII 335 [364-365]).

Schloss was later murdered in Dachau, which became another "Nazi atrocity". In the prosecution discussion of the Schloss murder, it is never mentioned that he was a sexual attacker of children; instead it was implied that Schloss was killed for being Jewish, and for no other reason (Document 664-PS, XXVI 174-187).

No causal nexus was ever shown between Streicher, Frank or Rosenberg's anti-Semitic beliefs and the commission of any crime; nor was it proven that the crime involved (i.e., the so-called "Holocaust") was ever even committed. This was assumed, and Streicher's writings were assumed to have helped "cause" it.

Streicher made several "highly improper" remarks which were stricken from the record, and for which he was admonished, with the consent of his attorney, Dr Marx. One of these remarks has been deleted after the fifth paragraph of page 310 of volume XII of the typeset transcript [page 337, line 30 of the German], but may be found on pages 8494-5 of the mimeographed transcript. Streicher said:

"If I might finish now with a description of my own life, it will be with the description of an experience which will show you, gentlemen, of the Tribunal, that without the government's wanting it, things may happen which are not human, not according to the principles of humanity.

"Gentlemen, I was arrested, and during my internment I experienced things such as we, the Gestapo, have been accused of. For four days I was without clothes in a cell. I was burned; I was thrown on the floor; and an iron chain was put upon me. I had to kiss the feet of Negroes who spit in my face. Two coloured men and a white officer spit in my mouth, and when I didn't open it any more, they opened it with a wooden stick, and when I asked for water I was led to the latrine and I was ordered to drink from there.

"In Wiesbaden, gentlemen, a doctor took pity, and I state here a Jewish director of the hospital acted correctly. I state here, in order not to be misunderstood, the Jewish officers who are guarding us here in prison have acted correctly, and doctors who also treat me have even been considerate. And you may see from this statement the contrast from that prison until this moment."

Another "improper remark" has been deleted after the first paragraph on page 349 of volume XII [page 379 in German], and appears in the mimeographed transcript on page 8549:

"So as to avoid a misunderstanding, I have to say that I was beaten in Freising so much and for days without clothes that I have lost forty per cent of my hearing capacity and people are laughing when I ask. I can't help it that I was treated like that. Therefore, I ask to hear the question again."

To which Lt. Col. Griffith-Jones replied:

"I can show it to you and we'll repeat the question as loud as you want it."

Since this was a matter within Streicher's personal knowledge, and not hearsay, it is difficult to see why the remarks were stricken, while hearsay favourable to the prosecution was retained (indeed, the prosecution case consists of little else beside oral and written hearsay). If the prosecution did not believe Streicher's testimony that he had been tortured, they were free to cross-examine him for inconsistencies and to show that he was lying; instead, he was simply admonished, and the passages stricken. So much for truth, justice, and a fair trial.

Streicher claimed that his demands for the "extermination" of Jewry were mostly brought about by the bombing raids and calls for extermination of the German people from the other side;

"If in America an author called Erich Kauffman [correct: Theodore Kaufman] can publicly demand that all men in Germany capable of fathering children should be sterilised, for the purpose of exterminating the German people, then I say, eye for eye and tooth for tooth. This is a theoretical literary matter." (XII 366 [398-399]). (V 91-119 [106-137]; XII 305-416 [332-453]; XVIII 190-220 [211-245]).

www.ingramcontent.com/pod-product-compliance
Lightning Source LLC
Chambersburg PA
CBHW020021050426
42450CB00005B/586